OZARK HOWLER

K.W. Peery

10/06/17

GenZPublishing.org

Aberdeen, NJ

ISBN: 9780692889329

DEDICATION

To: Jen Anderson-Peery

My love and most trusted accomplice

Special Thanks...

Tim Winborn, co-writer of "Wetlands"

Cover artwork by Bruce McClain

TABLE OF CONTENTS

CONFISCATED

The Oklahoma State Troopers
confiscated our contraband
on Saint Patrick's Day...2006

I was wheelin' a rented Lincoln
and Kenny was ridin' shotgun
We thought travelin' after midnight
would be our best bet...
-n- we were wrong

Just three miles North
of Thackerville
we could see a set of headlights
closin' fast in our rearview

Kenny tossed a "J"
out the passenger side window
as I eased off...from Eighty-Five
and tried to get my shit
together

About that time...
my cellphone rang
It was Juanita from Waco
and I didn't have time to talk

As the trooper went disco
I pulled swiftly onto the shoulder
and tried my best to act sober

Two hours later...
we made it to Texas
with an empty trunk
and barely enough cash
for gas

Who could've guessed
Okie Troopers would be so eager
to play "Let's Make A Deal"
at 4:20 in the mornin'

SONNY & NOT CHER'S

She said she wanted
to take me home
and make me
breakfast in bed

My Wife had filed
for divorce that afternoon
so I thought...
what the hell

I'd been sittin'
at Sonny & Not Cher's
since 6PM
listenin' to Waylon songs
on the jukebox

Beyond a single row
of well-worn pool tables
the High Life clock
read 12:22AM

So I poured another
lukewarm beer
from the pitcher
and ran my left hand
along her fishnet covered thighs

She was at least forty
and way outta my league
I knew I'd have to pitch
a perfect game

As the bartender cried...
LAST CALL
I ordered two shots of
Wild Turkey 101

When we pulled into
her driveway
she said...
I'll bet you like your eggs
over easy

Coincidentally...her name was Cher
The eggs were scrambled
And four days later...I found out
Sonny was her ex-husband

BLUETICK

My Grandpa Wayne
had two prize winnin'
Bluetick Coonhounds
while I was growin' up

Bo was built
like a brick shithouse
and usually stayed close to home...
unless the neighbors Treein' Walker
was in heat

His brother...Oop...
was just the opposite
Born to run 24/7...
I loved countin' the ribs
on his skinny frame...
when he'd slink in
for some of Grandma's
gravy soaked table scraps

Bo was as gentle as
an evenin' rain in August
And on hot summer nights
you'd see him wadin'
with the Holsteins
at the edge of Grandpa's pond

Oop was always on the mend
for one reason or another
He loved chasin' grain trucks
during harvest
and he said it kept him
in good fightin' shape
all winter long

Bo died first...
from natural causes
at the ripe old age of seventeen

Oop...disappeared shortly after
and never returned home

11

Some of the Old Timers said
he probably died from loneliness

I prefer to believe...
that ole Oop ran off
with Bo's girlfriend
and lived fat in his final days

COTTONMOUTH

The night I almost drowned...
we were runnin' trotlines
on Big Muddy

Our ole flat-bottom Jon
was powered by a 1950's era
Phantom Pflueger trollin' motor
that we'd rigged to run
on a 12-volt battery

High on amphetamines...
-n- crudely dialin' back our dose
We took sporadic snorts
from a fresh fifth
of Kentucky Gentleman

I was unfit to dive
the way I did
And I'll certainly never forget
the few panic filled moments
I felt...just prior to resurfacin'

We caught twelve flatheads...
-n- two snappin' turtles
 And had to shoot one
overly aggressive cottonmouth
with Johnny's...Ruger 10/22

I filleted the fish shoreside...
while Jim released the snappers

Two days later...
Johnny crafted a custom
cottonmouth hatband...

I still wear it sometimes
just to remind me
what dancin' with death
looks like
in the rearview

UTILITY PLAYER

I'm a switch-hittin'
Base-stealin'
Beer-drinkin'
Son of a baseball player

Right field...
Left field...
Second base...
Ready whenever they need me

I'm a belly-slidin'
Pitch-grindin'
Shit-talkin'
Utility player

They called me up
from Omaha
on a swelterin' July day
and I went three for four

Stole two
Walked once
and told the opposing catcher
I screwed his wife the night before

I'm a utility player
A journeyman
An odds-beater
And a genuine wild card...
when October rolls around

JETTISONED

I filled an old Rubbermaid tub
with letters from lovers
and dreams of things
I'll never share

Ya know...
some stuff simply survives
because I'm sentimental
And others I wish I'd saved
were hastily jettisoned...
twenty or so years ago

Like the night I threw
my footlocker off the
Peabody Hotel in Memphis
convinced those damn ducks
were plotting my premature demise

Or that time...on the corner
of Oregon and El Cajon
when I was almost outta bread
and traded a stack of Topps
for a fifth of Tanqueray

I've collected more contraband
than I care to disclose
as I'm certain the statute of limitations
does not apply to my specific situation

I've been called
a rake...a rogue...and a rambler...
Always ready
to jettison any and all evidence
at a moment's notice

I filled an old Rubbermaid tub
with letters from lovers
and naked pictures
taken in places I may
not see again...

Until the next time around

15

DALE

The night Dale got pinched
for that botched bank job in Joplin
he was drivin' my Grandpa's
Laredo tan...73 Fleetwood

It had bald tires...
expired tags
and just enough fuel to burn
most the evidence

Down on his luck...
-n- trollin' for an easy score
Dale had made a deal with the Devil
many moons before

He had seven sticks of dynamite
a fifth of Evan Williams
and an old double barrel shotgun
scrounged up from somewhere
in Grandpa's barn

They say...when the State Troopers
finally hunted him down
Dale was just seventeen miles South
of the Iowa line

It was the 16th of November
in 1989...
Dale was sentenced to twenty-two years
in the Missouri State Pen

I still remember the tears
in my Grandpa's eyes
when we took the insurance check
to deposit at Investors Federal

Three days later...
while doin' chores
my Grandpa found
a blue duffel bag

stuffed under a stack
of empty Pioneer sacks

It held twenty-six thousand dollars
in twenties...tens and fives
-n- my Grandpa spent it all
on a new Franchi 12-gauge
and tricked out
Palomino Gold...Olds 442

PROFOUND SADNESS

Profound sadness
smells like rain
As an unmerciful March
snuffs out
yet another invisible hero

And the only shred of hope
left clinging to tomorrow
is what survives
this curtain call
of suffering and silence

Ben was born into the World
with a love...infused with light—
That's essential when braving
this brand of darkness

Tempered in tragedy...
-n- tested by turmoil
It's the same ole blistered trigger finger
that claims twenty-two souls a day

Profound sadness
smells like rain
Where nothing really explains
the depth of helplessness

Or the weight of imagined Freedom...
Ben proudly carried
as a man willing to sacrifice everything...
in an effort to show his scars
Sophisticated shards...
are embedded in salvation
As Ben's spirit transcends...
all earthly understanding

SHEP

There was a Beechnut pouch
on the cracked dash
of his '58 Ford Fairlane

You could see spit stains
tricklin' down the
driver's side door

He would sit
in the parkin' lot
of Piggly Wiggly

Listenin' to Elmore James
"One Way Out"...
on chrome cassette

Born in Memphis...
and bound to the bottle
Ole Shep lived the blues

We'd usually shoot the shit
about R.L. Burnside
while sippin' Booker's
from my Grandpa's hip flask

Shep would always say…
"Can you spot me a Franklin...
I might need better bail...
down in Biloxi"

MYSTICAL MARTYRDOM

I'm vehemently opposed
to mystical martyrdom
So I celebrate most Fat Tuesday's
down at Joe's Standard

And for good measure...
I typically order a double Maker's
to reinforce the truth
that's slowly sinkin'...
like the silky head
on this damn Guinness draught

Then...on Ash Wednesday
I plan to please
my hellacious hangover...
with greasy pork steaks
cooked over Kingsford...
on a classic Weber kettle

And while enjoyin' a Parodi cigar
I'll listen to Smokey & the Miracles
sing "Tears of a Clown"
Still wonderin' why Marvin's Dad
had to gun him down
in the Spring of '84

WAITS

She said—
It's too hard to dance
to a Tom Waits song
especially when his pianos
been drinkin' in Minneapolis
since Saint Patrick's Day

So on the corner of 9th Street
and Hennepin
you can still hear
a sad slide trombone
and the talk of tragedy...
trackside at Canterbury Park

She said—
He called her collect from Istanbul
on a Wednesday mornin' at 3AM
Softly singin' "Gun Street Girl"
while wearin'...worn-out Alligator shoes
and Hai Karate after shave

Now workin'...in a Waukegan whorehouse
at Apache and West Greenwood
She spins Little Anthony and the Imperials...
on a stolen record player
wonderin' why the blues
always seem bluer...when Tom calls

22-33-44

You could hear
my death rattle
in June of '95

An honorable discharge
from the Navy
just four days after
my 22nd birthday

Ya know...
Divorce has never been
a four-letter word
But it sure as Hell
should be

You could hear
my Cheyne-Stokes
in March of '06

Affectionately referred to as...
the dawn of my deepest darkness
A midlife crisis...if you will
At the ripe old age of 33

Stoned in Speegleville
Drinkin' the High Life
Spendin' more on speed
than an Earnhardt...
just days before Daytona

You can hear the screams...
in my ravaged dreams
Only months from 44

I've got miles of scars
embedded in my liver
That's sure to shock
even the most calloused
medical examiner

So all you haters...
should certainly stay tuned

while I attempt to cheat the odds
and dance with my dealer
for at least another decade

BARBEQUE

Catfish said...
he heard
Kansas City's known
for beautiful women
and barbeque

I replied...
Better known for barbeque
than beautiful women

But at my age
I'll still slather on the spicy...
while ordering a signature side
from a beautifully built
blonde or brunette

Ya know...
My ole burnt ends
barely have time to discriminate

SKUNK BEAR

I crossed paths
with a Skunk Bear
fourteen miles
northeast of Anchorage
on the Knik arm of Cook Inlet

He was sprayin' his scent
near the base of a
black cottonwood tree
and for a moment
I was mesmerized

His short snout...was sniffin' the air
like a full fat kid...
in summer school
after polishin' off a swollen can
of Van Camp's Pork N' Beans

The Nasty Cats...
stocky swagger
somewhat startled me
as I reached for
my Fifty-Six Leica

Zoomin' in
on his razor sharp claws
I snapped a few...just in time
to capture him...flashin' me...
his scarred middle finger

HUNTER

December 26th, 1991...
Continental flight 1414
out of Minneapolis—
Saint Paul

I was sippin' hot black coffee...
while watchin' sleet
bounce off
our starboard wing

As a stranger
sittin' beside me asked...
"Where ya headed kid"
I replied...San Diego...

He flagged down
a long legged...
flight attendant
to pour another double Makers

Shufflin' ink soaked pages...
while mumblin' softly to himself
I suddenly recognized the character
and began thinkin' of unique ways
to engage him

He reminded me of every
dream I never had
And in that moment
all I could think to ask
were superficial questions
with no guts...grit or gravitas

As we landed in California...
Hunter handed me his card
Words...in blood red...
on thick cover stock

He said...
"If you ever need an alibi...
have them call me"

I still carry his card...
as a reminder
of how hauntingly humble
greatness really is

MENTORS

Most of my mentors
are already dead...or dyin'
I guess that's what happens
when rows get short
and the reaper appears

Scattered shards....
of studio sessions spent
piss-drunk on Booker's
usually pushin' too hard...
to scramble another hit

Most of my mentors
are already dead...or dyin'
So that explains this symphony
of sensational voices...
Singin' Son Volt at 3AM

Warm hiss...
Half inch...
3M analog
A hi-hat splash...
-n- hybrid Fender squall

Most of my mentors
are already dead...or dyin'
So please line up...
and share some sage advice
While his footsteps close the distance

THE KINGS CODEINE

Perhaps the last thing
on Elvis Presley's mind was...
"Damn...I could've had a V8"

The King expired...
near his throne
On August 16th, 1977

Time of death...2PM Central

An autopsy was performed...
that determined the cause of death
as...cardiac arrhythmia

Toxicology reports later identified
a cocktail of drugs...
prescribed by "Doctor Nick"...
that included Quaaludes...
Demerol...Dilaudid...
Valium...Percodan…Phenobarb...
Cocaine and Codeine

The King's codeine intake was found
to be at ten times...therapeutic level

With a plethora of pills and powder
prescribed...
Elvis had been severely constipated...
for over four months
He had ballooned to almost 350 pounds

So was he really trying to kill himself at age
fourty-two...
All objective evidence certainly suggests it

Priscilla had left him...
and taken Lisa Marie
He was too fat and sick to
go back out on the road

Elvis always surrounded himself
with people determined to manipulate

and control the flow of cash...
no matter the cost

So instead of having a refreshing V8...
on that warm August afternoon
The King decided
to take more than he should...
one final time

OFF THE RECORD

We met Cobain...
Off The Record
in San Diego
Circa '91...

My buddy Scott
convinced me to
roll along that afternoon

Fresh off the farm...
I had no idea who he was
or how a fourty-minute set
could prove to be so instrumental

My friend was killed
in an accident
off the I-5
in February of '94

Kurt made his
grand escape...
fifty-four days later

It's been twenty-three years -n- change
since we buried Scott in Atlanta
And not a day goes by...
that I don't think of them

MY VOICE

I found my voice...
in the blacktop grooves
on Route 139...
just North of Meadville

I drowned my voice...
on a wobbly barstool
at the Corner Pocket tavern...
while listenin' to Hag...
sing a Lefty song

I found my voice...
tied to a green metal chair
at the Speed Queen Laundromat
off Oregon street...near El Cajon

I drowned my voice...
on the ragin' Guadalupe
Back in '07...
In the midst
of my most manic meltdown

How far will I go...
and what will I be thinkin'
when it happens again

Oh...probably the same thing
I was thinkin' last time…
while staggerin' slowly...
along that ole ragged-ass edge...
I've been cheatin' for the past fourty-four years

DRAM

I enjoy a smooth dram...
every now and then
Ya know...
my marination process
is variable

Like Dead Sea swimmers...
in February
Or spring training win records...
down in Surprise Arizona

So I'll give cheers...
with aged Glenlivet
For every explosion...
off Hosmer's...Dove Tail Maple Bat

Then pour an extra special dram...
to toast all those dark-horse writers...
who started too late...
or gave up too soon

TWENTY-THREE

I made a deal with my demons...
somewhere South of Saint Louis...
on the Sixth of June...in a thunderstorm

My nerves were shot...
tires bald...
in a Bahama blue...Ford Ranchero

Out of powder...
-n- scroungin' for pills
Desperate for anything...
to carry me back to Memphis

Where bad beef barbecue
-n- greasy blues...
were my only means of survival...
at the ripe old age of twenty-three

ELUSIVE ABSOLUTION

Fumes of tragedy linger
like love lost by the roadside
Manic emotions cycle...
as helplessness sets in

Where the intensity of white noise
is absolutely deafening
The weight of grief
engulfs everything I've ever known

Anxiety...Agony...and
Elusive Absolution

Suspended here...
in the vanishing vapor

K.W.Peery

FADED

Losin' control sometimes
is nothin' new
Hell...my first midlife crisis
visited at thirty-six

Anxiety is a wicked mistress
She'll tempt you with tactile precision
Then gut ya...in broad daylight

Make no mistake...
my sufferin' is subjective
As I attempt to enter the darkroom
there's always a flickerin' neon that says
"No survivors...beyond this point"

The grind can be exhaustin'
Isolation...while intermittent is problematic
Shit can sure go south in a hurry

Existence is certainly fragile
and it eclipses all rational explanation
The silver linin' in this godforsaken journey...
is unconditional love
It's been my only salvation

Faded, fragmented and forgiven

Despite my many flaws

CALCULATED

The risk seemed worth it
so I ordered another double
The Bartender smirked...
as she filled my glass

It was November 12th
"Deer Season" in Missouri
I loaded the jukebox...
with Haggard, Fogerty and Petty

The Brown Bear was nearly empty...
except for the usual suspects
I'd been drinkin' and druggin'
all afternoon

Nobody tells ya at twenty-seven...
that mistakes might cost more
I'd never been arrested...
even on the nights I should've been

If calculated risks were a specialty...
I was convinced I'd earned a PhD
As Petty sang Refugee...
the Adderall was wearin' off

My head was poundin'...
as I jammed another twenty in
Playin' more Croce...and Tom T…
this time around
A Falstaff clock was showin' 8:15PM....
I was beyond three sheets
The best moves weren't in my playbook...
as I started jabberin'

Things escalated quickly...
It was barstools...bourbon and shattered glass
The law was called...
as I made my way out a side door into the alley
My silver Eldorado was parked down the block
I thought I was home free...

But as I turned onto St. Joe Avenue...
all the lights went out

I was cool...cuffed -n- calculated...
as Judge Wilson set my bail

SINISTER ELEMENTS

As the poor beg for mercy
A rich man waits in the wings
Like a vulture circling
It's only a matter of time
The votes were cast
Big money wins
There's no stay of execution
Another Inauguration Day is imminent

Fooled again
Sleight of hand
Circus tricks
And a marching band
Step on up
Pledge your allegiance
The sinister elements
Have long since beat us

There's clearly no difference
For us workin'-class stiffs
We'll suffer together
In the same fate as the previous sixteen
And if you think Corporations care
You're playin' right into their hands
Beware what ya ask for...

Fooled again
Sleight of hand
Circus tricks
And a marching band
Step on up
Pledge your allegiance
The sinister elements
Have long since beat us

Yeah...the sinister elements
Have already beat us

JUNE AFTERNOON

We bought three cases of the "High Life"
on our way South that mornin'
and stopped just North of Sedalia
to ice them down in Dad's big orange cooler

My Brother had just been hired on
with the Union Pacific
and I'd finally graduated from college...
thanks to the G.I. Bill

There was always an open invitation
at Aunt Mary's house...
so we thought it was a perfect time to visit

Still clingin' to my twenties...
I was anxious for the next chapter in my life
I can remember thinkin'...
damn...I'm gettin' old

Nobody since John Wayne
was tougher than my little Brother Peeve...
A hard workin' son of a gun...since the day he
turned three...
Hell...he'd been chewin' plug tobacco regularly
since five

I'll never forget the mornin' we arrived...
There was nobody home which was unusual
Especially since we called
to let her know we were comin' the day before

It was a Saturday...and already ten thirty
So we started livin' "The High Life" while we waited

About twenty minutes later...
her Blazer pulled off Grey Fox Road...
and rolled up the short gravel drive

She wore dark oversized shades
and all we could see was teeth…
Aunt Mary...our Mom's youngest Sister...
could've been cast as Sissy in Urban Cowboy...
or Annie Savoy in Bull Durham
As the driver door swung open...she said
"Hey Fella's...ya drinkin' without me?"
We just laughed and helped her into the house
with a truckload of groceries

After everything was put away...
She said...it's such a nice day...
let's sit outside

So in three lawn chairs we sat...
all afternoon
She drank Busch Light...
We had "The Champagne of Beers"
Swappin' stories about Grandma -n- Grandpa...
Thomas Hill Lake...
and how we'd spend all the money...
if we hit the Lottery that night

It was a perfect June afternoon...
Perhaps the most meaningful I've ever had

FARM KITCHEN

There was an old Corning Ware dish
of homemade applesauce...
next to a pea green Melmac plate
with leftover minute steaks...

A hint of biscuits still in the air
but no evidence of any survivors

Grandpa's Realistic radio
gave an abbreviated farm market report
A stack of Daily Tribune's were
neatly placed on Grandma's
black retro step-stool in the corner

Their Roper gas stove
still radiatin' heat...
held two cast iron skillets...
One was clean...
the other half full of lukewarm milk gravy
An old percolator sat in the back...
like a shy kid in Sunday school
The oak kitchen door had slender windows...
It was propped open with a cloth-covered brick
to let the heat escape

You could hear the deep freezer's compressor
rattle out a symphony on the finished back porch
Their Sixties linoleum pattern was tiny bricks
placed together...
They looked like jigsaw puzzle pieces
It was August...
I was starvin'
so I sat down to eat
just minutes before
I heard Grandpa's Ford
comin' up the long gravel drive

DEAD OF WINTER

There's an indescribable emptiness
in the dead of winter
that weakens my resolve
It's passive suffering...
Like a full flask in a dyin' mans vest pocket
His cold...chapped lips of Spanish blue
thirst for something to kill the pain...
but he no longer has the strength to swallow

In the dead of winter...
this Missouri wind
can cut a swath from my exposed skin...
like a sickle bar mower through Summer fescue
So I dress in layers...
of Carhartt...wool and leather
Spendin' more than I ever thought possible
on designer coffee and fuckin' heated seats
in my new Escalade

In the dead of winter...
I call my folks who've retired to South Florida...
only when I feel guilty
Because I don't wanna be reminded
of how cold it really is in February...
or how goddamned stupid I am for stayin' here

There's an indescribable emptiness
in the dead of winter
that only a glutton for punishment can fully
comprehend...
So I belly up to the bar for another shot of
Jameson...
and toast that poor dyin' bastard
who's too frozen to freeze and too cold to care

LEROY

I handed my glass to Miller...
then sucker punched Leroy
off a barstool at the Friendly Tavern
It was November as I remember...
we had been drinkin' all day
and makin' the rounds

Leroy was known around town...
as a tough ass biker
and no count son of a bitch
He tried to start shit with three or four others...
before findin' me
He professed his love for Hitler...
among other things…
I never took my eyes off the eight ball

Leroy wouldn't leave it alone
He began insulting my flat top
and the Military...
It went on like this for at least another hour…
I never uttered a word
After three more beers
and a half dozen shots...
I was ready to rumble
so I struck him...
just above the left eyebrow

According to Miller...
Leroy's heels were at eye level...
before he hit the hardwood floor in disbelief

We were already in the street when he came out
blood tricklin' like water from a busted jailhouse
shitter

The cops were called
We were banned indefinitely
Miller took the back roads home
Three weeks later the Friendly caught fire
I never crossed paths with Leroy again

THE STREETS

The streets are dark
damp and dangerous
Young pimps sit in aging Cadillac's
countin' their stacks of cash
while trollin' for fresh talent...

Kansas City is ripe for young hustlers...
sportin' expensive shoes
and cheap automatic weapons

Heavy on hungry...
always lookin' for the next easy score
but there's nothin' easy anymore...

On the greedy side of this City
only the lucky survive

The streets are dark
damp and dangerous

Ravaged by murder...
where corruption is still King
The Royals are winners again
and the hookers work overtime...
whether the Chiefs make the playoffs or not

SLAUGHTERHOUSE

Slaughterhouse hooks
carry suffering tongues
heavy hearts and a fatty liver

Meanwhile...
calloused fingers tremble
fueled by adrenaline...
stained in fresh blood

The overflowing gut barrels ripen
in ninety-degree heat
Waitin' on a fat yellow cat
to stop licking his chops...
long enough to realize...
he might be next

The butcher smells money...
His season never ends
It's raw hamburger
on stale saltines for breakfast
and despite his cholesterol...
he prefers his steak...
chicken fried with extra gravy

It's a fuckin' slaughterhouse...
There aren't any rules
Just busted knuckles...
his bad back
and a thirst for something he can't quite explain

K.W.Peery

OZARK HOWLER

Southeast of Greenview
Way back in the timber
It was a little after dark
On the Thirteenth of November
Bill was on the shotgun
I carried a Hogleg Smith
We only caught a glimpse
And ain't been back there since

He was big as a mountain grizzly bear
And ripe as a shithouse skunk
That damned ole Ozark Howler
Scared us uphill to the truck

Never seen nothin' like it
Don't need to see him again
That damned ole Ozark Howler
Spooked us clean out of our skin

Yeah…that damned ole Ozark Howler
Won't ever catch us there again

My Grandpa went out fishin'
One night on Indian Creek
It was long about Midnight
When he caught his first peek
Claimed he tried to lure him
With a treble and two sardines
Said he nearly crapped his pants
When that bastard let out a scream

He was big as a mountain grizzly bear
And ripe as a shithouse skunk
That damned ole Ozark Howler
Scared us uphill to the truck

Never seen nothin' like it
Don't need to see him again
That damned ole Ozark Howler
Spooked us clean out of our skin

Yeah...that damned ole Ozark Howler
Won't ever catch us there again

HILLBILLY HIGH

The gas ran out
Here in the house
Burnin' hedge posts
Since this mornin'
My neck is stiff
And I can barely lift
This head off
The checkered floorin'

I got Hillbilly High...
Last Saturday night
Now it's four
On Wednesday mornin'
Who woulda thunk
I couldn't handle this drunk
They say...Moonshine's
Seldom borin'

So it's a line of smash
Through some rolled up cash
Livin' free...
Means almost dyin'
I got Hillbilly High...
Last Saturday night
Now it's four
On Wednesday mornin'

The Sheriff says
My truck is his
He towed it
Since I've got warrants
So I called my Ex
For the weekly sex
But she swapped me
For a dude named Warren

I got Hillbilly High...
Last Saturday night
Now it's four
On Wednesday mornin'
Who woulda thunk
I couldn't handle this drunk
They say...Moonshine's
Seldom borin'

So it's a line of smash
Through some rolled up cash
Livin' free...
Means almost dyin'
I got Hillbilly High...
Last Saturday night
Now it's four
On Wednesday mornin'

Yeah...it's quarter past five
-n- I'm barely alive
Still Hillbilly High...
This mornin'

DEAD MAN

Hillbilly crank
And a new tattoo
Trunk full of liquor
In his 442
Light on money
Heavy on speed
Got a full tank of gas
And some high-powered weed

Think what ya want
-n- do as you please
Cause nobody knows
What a Dead Man sees
It's a long shot bet
In a whorehouse squeeze
Yeah...nobody knows
What a Dead Man needs

Cause nobody wants...
What a Dead Man sees

Pushin' the limits
On sanity's rails
He's been here before
Crazier than Hell
It's five in the chamber
Blood on the streets
An Ozark smirk
In the passenger seat

Think what ya want
-n- do as you please
Cause nobody knows
What a Dead Man sees
It's a long shot bet
In a whorehouse squeeze

Yeah...nobody knows
What a Dead Man needs

Cause nobody wants...
What a Dead Man sees

EIGHTY-EIGHT DEVILLE

Pearl white
Plush grey seats
A Delco deck
That liked to repeat
Room in the trunk
For our contraband
Seventy-One South
With a hundred grand

Runnin' from trouble
Just me -n- Wild Bill
A fifth of Evan Williams
In an Eighty-Eight DeVille
It was three days after Christmas
Circa...Ninety-Five
An Eighty-Eight DeVille...
Tryin' to stay alive

In my Eighty-Eight DeVille
Somehow we survived

We hit a bank in Hamilton
Late that afternoon
Then slid over to Winston
Knowin' Hell was comin' soon
Broke South...that evenin'
It was cold and freezin' rain
Desperate...drunk -n- loaded
Too numb to feel the pain

Runnin' from trouble
Just me -n- Wild Bill
A fifth of Evan Williams
In an Eighty-Eight DeVille
It was three days after Christmas

Circa...Ninety-Five
In an Eighty-Eight DeVille...
Tryin' to stay alive

In my Eighty-Eight DeVille
Somehow we survived

Headed East from Joplin
On a solid sheet of ice
Spun her around three times
Chasin' our headlights
Wheels locked up...-n- loaded
Bill never spilled a drop
Safe -n- sound in Springfield...
We never saw a Cop

Runnin' from trouble
Just me -n- Wild Bill
A fifth of Evan Williams
In my Eighty-Eight DeVille
It was three days after Christmas
Circa...Ninety-Five
In an Eighty-Eight DeVille...
Tryin' to stay alive

In my Eighty-Eight DeVille
Somehow we survived

FLATHEAD

After the flood
Back in '81
I'd go flathead fishin'
With my Uncle Don
Usin' chicken livers
We'd soaked in the Sun
The Salt River Basin
Was a lot of fun

He drove a red Silverado
Drank Busch from a can
Used treble hooks
-n- was a hell of a man
Served in Korea...
Till '53
He loved flathead fishin'
And schoolin' me

They were still there workin'
On the Cannon Dam
Before floodin' the flats
Where we liked to stand
Don worked for the State
And knew all the guys
One evenin' we toured
All the guts inside

He drove a red Silverado
Drank Busch from a can
Used treble hooks
-n- was a hell of a man
Served in Korea...
Till '53
He loved flathead fishin'
And schoolin' me

I'll never forget
All the lessons I learned
Before Mark Twain lake
Covered our berm
Still laugh out loud
When I think of him
More than an Uncle...
Don was my friend

He drove a red Silverado
Drank Busch from a can
Used treble hooks
-n- was a hell of a man
Served in Korea...
Till '53
He loved flathead fishin'
And schoolin' me

ABILENE BOX

There's an Abilene box
That holds old treasure
Dog tags...ribbons...
Medals and letters
Saved by a Man
With War on his mind
Claims he went crazy
At least three times

Deep in the hills
You can still hear him holler
An Abilene Box
And a moonshine swaller
Haunted by memories
Tamin' old beasts
An Abilene Box
Too shattered for sleep

An Abilene Box...
And the secrets he keeps

Sits in his truck
With bootleg cassettes
Campbell...Clapton...
Gibbons...and Betts
At home with the lonely
In an Ozark cocoon
Stays high most nights
Sleeps in past Noon

Deep in the hills
You can still hear him holler
An Abilene Box
And a moonshine swaller
Haunted by memories
Tamin' old beasts

An Abilene Box
Too shattered for sleep

An Abilene Box...
And the secrets he keeps

ASHTRAY ROSES

Harnessin' lightnin'
Waitin' for rain
The voices inside
Sound kinda strange
Bukowski at midnight
Collins at three
When transformers arc
It terrifies me

Roses in the ashtray
Hurt on the vine
A bottle of port
And nothin' but time
Black Sparrow feathers
In wingtip shoes
Roses in the ashtray
Thinkin' about you

Yeah roses in the ashtray...
Port wine...-n- blues

Poets past forty
Suffer and bleed
Tippin' their hand
So the thin wolves can feed
There's an old velvet painting
Of a worn out King
A spent cigarette
-n- our wedding rings

Roses in the ashtray
Hurt on the vine
A bottle of port
And nothin' but time
Black Sparrow feathers
In wingtip shoes

60

Roses in the ashtray
Thinkin' about you

Yeah roses in the ashtray...
Port wine...-n- blues

GREENVILLE

I shot a man on Front street
In Greenville late last night
He hit me with a pool cue
And that wasn't very bright
The radio says I'm wanted
A manhunt -n- APB
I can hear copters overhead
Their hounds are chasin' me

There was gunfire in Greenville
Three rounds from a Forty-Five
Gunfire in Greenville
Now I'm runnin' for my life

Gunfire in Greenville
Where prayin' won't do no good
There was gunfire in Greenville
Now I'm out here in the woods

I threw my cell down a well
When I decided to cut -n- run
Now the GPS...is my best bet
Got a rifle and two shotguns
Wasn't lookin' to hurt nobody
But trouble sure found my ass
Now I'm ten miles South of Greenville
And the sun's sure sinkin' fast

There was gunfire in Greenville
Three rounds from a Forty-Five
Gunfire in Greenville
Now I'm runnin' for my life

Gunfire in Greenville
Where prayin' won't do no good

There was gunfire in Greenville
Now I'm out here in the woods

Yeah...there was gunfire in Greenville
And prayers won't do no good

BITTER SOMETIMES

I get bitter sometimes
When wicked wins
Too much tequila
Or just enough gin

I get bitter sometimes
In February
When the wind won't lay
And the roads are scary

I get bitter sometimes
When my alarm clock rings
Waitin' on coffee
Among other things

I get bitter sometimes
When rejections roll in
Alone in my bunker
Beginnin' again

I get bitter sometimes
With the daily news
Stirrin' up hatred
Killin' my mood

I get bitter sometimes
When things unravel
My mind plays tricks
On the days I'm frazzled

I get bitter sometimes
When the words won't come
My refractory period
Now a longer one

I get bitter sometimes
When posers unite
To push their agenda
Despite what's right

I get bitter sometimes
In city traffic

So I crank the blues
Cause it calms my panic

I get bitter sometimes
When I see others suffer
Alone in silence
Our Sisters -n- Brothers

I get bitter...sometimes

MARROW

This cold air is a bastard
I'm gettin' too damn old
To expose myself this way
-n- that's how my story goes
Been headed the wrong direction
Down a lonesome...crooked road
A Bible on the bench seat...
Next to my Old Crow

This marrow that protects my body
Don't have no place to go
-n- the prayers...I said yesterday
They ain't takin' hold
Made a bad deal with the Devil
Now the Lord's all I've got left
Down deep in the marrow
Where this pain won't let me rest

Yeah...deep in the marrow's
The only hope I've got left

Lost in weak transmission
These ole frozen power lines
Tryin' almost anything
That'll allow me to unwind
Got a station outta Brunswick
Playin' Hank's "...Lovesick Blues"
Ten miles West of Macon
Needin' more than classic tunes

This marrow that protects my body
Don't have no place to go
-n- the prayers I said yesterday
They ain't takin' hold
Made a bad deal with the devil
Now the Lord's all I've got left

Down deep in the marrow
Where this pain won't let me rest

Yeah...deep in the marrow's
The only hope I've got left

SENTIMENTAL

Feelin's washin' in
Like waves on Mission Beach
Ten toes in the sand...
Just watchin' my castle sink
Sentimental sounds...
Surroundin' Crystal Pier
As the tide rolls out...
I'm wishin' you were here

Alone in San Diego...
Three years since ya passed
I'm feelin' sentimental...
Listenin' to Rosanne Cash
Got a red-eye booked this evenin'
Baby...back to Baton Rouge
Spreadin' your ashes in the sand
I'm sure ya would approve

Yeah...feelin' sentimental
I'm not the same here without you

I'll never forget Point Loma
In the Spring of Ninety-Two
Ya flew out to surprise me
-n- we never left the room
Cheap wine and waffles
Were all I could afford
Haze gray...-n- Navy pay
Rollin' pennies across the floor

Alone in San Diego...
Three years since ya passed
I'm feelin' sentimental...
Listenin' to Rosanne Cash
Got a red eye booked this evenin'
Baby...back to Baton Rouge

Spreadin' your ashes in the sand
I'm sure ya would approve

Yeah...feelin' sentimental
I'm not the same here without you

PIKEVILLE PETE

Hedge in his fireplace
Heads on the wall
A John Wayne movie
In his overalls
Booker's bourbon
From a dented flask
Won't share a sip
No need to ask

Pikeville Pete…
Plays Kentucky blues
He's a Hillbilly Sage
In worn-out shoes
Smokes burley tobacco
In a briar pipe
Pikeville Pete...
Is the silent type

Yeah...Ole Pikeville Pete
He's the silent type

Likes homemade biscuits
With blackberry jam
Sunnyside eggs
And country ham
Sits on his porch
Till it's too dark to read
Claims a Bluetick Hound
Is the best of breed

Pikeville Pete...
Plays Kentucky blues
He's a Hillbilly Sage
In worn-out shoes
Smokes burley tobacco
In a briar pipe

Pikeville Pete...
Is the silent type

Yeah...Ole Pikeville Pete
He's the silent type

SUCKER'S BET

Gangster politicians
-n- Wall Street cheats
Stackin' the deck
After buyin' us cheap
Spendin' Chinese cash
For a wall on the border
Every pimp hand played
Breeds civil disorder

Listen up hustlers
We're not dead yet
It's time to tilt the odds
On this old Sucker's Bet
There's hate in our history
And blood-soaked streets
Smart money says...
We ain't quite beat

Yeah...Sucker's Bet regret
Seldom means we'll retreat

Billions of dirty dollars
Spent on division
Questionin' our fire
While fannin' religion
The business of Church
Is all sleight of hand
Trickin' the poor
While they pillage and brand

Listen up hustlers
We're not dead yet
It's time to tilt the odds
On this old Sucker's Bet
There's hate in our history
And blood-soaked streets

The smart money says
We ain't quite beat

Yeah...Sucker's Bet regret
Seldom means we'll retreat

Robber Baron Heirs
-n- War Profiteers
Pound the same drum
They've been poundin' for years
Countin' on silence
Always promisin' more
Slayin' our hopes
Then slammin' the door

Listen up hustlers
We're not dead yet
It's time to tilt the odds
On this old Sucker's Bet
There's hate in our history
And blood-soaked streets
The smart money says
We ain't quite beat

Yeah...Sucker's Bet regret
Seldom means we'll retreat

BALD ON GRAVEL

There's a calico cat
On my front porch
I think she's the neighbor's
But I'm not sure
Been up since five
Went to bed at three
My restless legs
Got the better of me

Feelin' reckless
Like bald on gravel
I'm frayed at the edges
-n- down right frazzled
Worn as a week
With no days off...
Like bald on gravel
I just can't stop

Yeah...I'm bald on gravel
-n- just can't stop

There's a Redbone Hound
Draggin' his chain
He's all souped-up
-n- actin' strange
Ready for a hunt
Been howlin' all week
Gonna cut his ass loose
So I can get some sleep

Feelin' reckless
Like bald on gravel
I'm frayed at the edges
-n- down right frazzled
Worn as a week
With no days off

Like bald on gravel
I just can't stop

Yeah...I'm bald on gravel
-n- just can't stop

HELL IN A HAT

A Seventy Riviera
In Gulfstream blue
Parked off Wayland
In West Plainview
We had plans to hit
The Centennial Bank
Me -n- ole Willie
And Fireball Frank

Mirrored sunglasses
We were Hell in a Hat
Deadly serious...
There was nothin' we lacked
They never saw us comin'
And ain't seen us since
We were Hell in a Hat
It was all offense

Yeah...Hell in a Hat
We were all offense

Frank was our wheelman
Willie a thinker
I could crack safes
With just two fingers
Our plan worked perfectly
On the Tenth of July
We stole seventy-eight grand
And nobody died

Mirrored sunglasses
We were Hell in a Hat
Deadly serious...
There was nothin' we lacked
They never saw us comin'
And ain't seen us since

We were Hell in a Hat
It was all offense

Yeah...Hell in a Hat
We were all offense

STUPOR

As unconscious echoes
Bounce and bleed
Raw devastation
Supersedes

Wide-awake...dreaming
In a constant state of shock
This circulatory collapse
With no hands on the clock

Manipulating ignorance
While drugging the truth
Is subtle sedation
In a smooth Vermouth

Executing innocence
Suffocating sheep
A sensational stupor...
Much deeper than sleep

RENO

Two tablespoons of codeine
-n- three parts tequila
Coltrane and cocaine
At the ole Turquoise Amoeba
A tall skinny hustler
Shootin' eight ball in the back
I saw him roll up earlier...
In a mirage Cadillac

Feelin' a little rough alright
In this Reno dressin' room
I made my way from Laughlin
Headed to Sacramento soon
The promoter says it's sold out
Two shows...back to back
I'm feelin' rough in Reno...
Mostly blue...with shades of black

Yeah...here I am in Reno
I might not make it back

Crooked lines off the dresser
I can hear the openin' act
My mind's off somewhere fishin'
A turkey feather in my hat
This ole red axe...is anxious
My fingers all limbered up
I stroll to the edge again...
Prayin' I did enough

Feelin' a little rough alright
In this Reno dressin' room
I made my way from Laughlin
Headed to Sacramento soon
The promoter says it's sold out
Two shows...back to back

I'm feelin' rough in Reno...
Mostly blue...with shades of black

Yeah...here I am in Reno
I might not make it back

SUNDAY

Well...they say I've got cancer
And my short rows...really numbered
My guts are full of gravel
It's slowly pullin' me under
So I sit here in the darkness
Punishin' my ragin' liver
A Zebco 808...
Dyin' here on ole Blue River

Now everyday is Sunday
As I struggle to tie my shoes
The ascites has taken over
This ole body that I've abused
Can't blame it on the whiskey
And I won't scream at GOD
Now everyday is Sunday
I'm cancer's lightnin' rod

Yeah...everyday is Sunday
I'm just cancer's lightnin' rod

Most mornin's I feel worthless
But that's really nothin' new
My bones are gettin' fragile
From all the chemo they like to use
So I try to tame this pain
With red wine, weed -n- song
And tell the folks I love
I'm sorry...I'm movin' on

Now everyday is Sunday
As I struggle to tie my shoes
The ascites has taken over
This ole body that I've abused
Can't blame it on the whiskey
And I won't scream at GOD

81

Now everyday is Sunday
I'm cancer's lightnin' rod

Yeah...everyday is Sunday
I'm just cancer's lightnin' rod

MEDGAR

Born in Decatur
The third of five
Medgar was made
To fight for what's right
He served in the Army
And somehow survived
At the Battle of Normandy
Where many men died

A Civil Rights Leader
Was slain in Jackson
With an Enfield rifle
And cowardly actions
Struck in the back...
Twenty-three...thirty-two
For thirty-seven years
He was bulletproof

Yeah…
He was slain in Jackson...
Fightin' for truth

Laid to rest...in Arlington
As his work marched on
Medgar was trained...
To strangle what's wrong
Justice prevailed...
In Ninety-Four
His Legacy intact...
Myrlie made sure

A Civil Rights Leader
Was slain in Jackson
With an Enfield rifle
And cowardly actions
Struck in the back

Twenty-three...thirty-two
For thirty-seven years
He was bulletproof

Yeah...
He was slain in Jackson...
Fightin' for truth

BUFFALO HIDES

As Plains Bison graze
On Tallgrass Prairie
Ghosts of Pawnee...
Seem solitary
The Blue Stem Hills
Have limestone guts
With prehistoric creatures
No plow could scuff

There are screams in dreams
Under overcast skies
As a Native drum beats
Over Buffalo Hides

Only take what they need
Twice a year...to survive
There are screams in dreams
Under overcast skies

Yeah...screams in dreams
Over Buffalo Hides

Where legendary nomads
Stalk their prey
Skinny coyotes
Usually lead the way
A Yellowboy Rifle
Holds fifteen rounds
In .44-40
That's plenty to...knock down

There are screams in dreams
Under overcast skies
As a Native drum beats
Over Buffalo Hides

Only take what they need
Twice a year...to survive
There are screams in dreams
Under overcast skies

Yeah...screams in dreams
Over Buffalo Hides

SNOWMAN

Seismic waves
And a Hillbilly high
Flat out pickin'
Ole Tony Rice
Dwight ridin' shotgun
Jimmy in the back
A freeborn man
Loves a smooth Cadillac

Rabbit made bail
-n- Possum's...on the run
Swamp Fox is fishin'...
Ain't catchin' none

Jerry Reed jamin'...
Croce's singin'..."Jim"
Where muddy water rolls
A Snowman can't swim

Yeah...ain't nobody say
A Snowman can swim

Up all night
Chasin' last week's pay
Lost this month's rent
And an ole Chevrolet
Lit my head on fire
Next to Charlie Rich
My last day sober
Was a son of a bitch

Rabbit made bail
-n- Possum's on the run
Swamp Fox is fishin'...
Ain't catchin' none

Jerry Reed jamin'
Croce's singin'..."Jim"
Where muddy water rolls
A Snowman can't swim

Yeah...ain't nobody say
A Snowman can swim

STAY

I stay strange...
Marginally kind
The delta awaits
My abstract mind
Where puddin' is proof
I've lived too long
Every day unnumbered
Is another swan song

I stay devoted...
Despite my rust
Most things I treasure
I had to dig up
I'm fourteen red
On the roulette wheel
And a fat stack of black
Next to ole Lucille

I stay bold...
In faded ink
Between the Worlds
Like a blind man's blink
My truth is sufferin'...
Nobody sees
Yeah...I gotta stay cool
Till the evil recedes

BEYOND BLUE NEON

Prescription pills
-n- medical bills
Same fox...
Slaughterin' my chickens
Career politicians
Cloaked in religion
Don't care about
Folks they're kickin'

Beyond bright-blue neon...
It's the same ole swingin' doors
Waitin' on somethin'...spiritual
Refusin' to be ignored
Listenin' to Gary Stewart
Whiskey trip...and a crooked line
Beyond bright-blue neon
I'm all souped up inside

Yeah...beyond the bright-blue neon
There ain't no place to hide

Spent my singles...
-n- had some Pringles
Drinkin' doubles
Down at Joe's
Short on smash...
Gotta make it last
For the sake
Of my crooked nose

Beyond bright-blue neon...
It's the same ole swingin' doors
Waitin' on somethin'...spiritual
Refusin' to be ignored
Listenin' to Gary Stewart
Whiskey trip...and a crooked line

Beyond bright-blue neon
I'm all souped up inside

Yeah...beyond the bright-blue neon
There ain't no place to hide

The Navy didn't need a Poet
Slingin' truth...-n- sellin' rhymes
Corpsman Up...I'm still bold enough
To share...what's on my mind

Beyond bright-blue neon...
It's the same ole swingin' doors
Waitin' on somethin'...spiritual
Refusin' to be ignored
Listenin' to Gary Stewart
Whiskey trip...and a crooked line
Beyond bright-blue neon
I'm all souped up inside

Yeah...beyond the bright-blue neon
There ain't no place to hide

SUICIDE KINGS

An inauguration of arrogance
Empty suits...and suicide kings
Evil cloaked in patriotism...
Fatted sheep...all ready to scream

Intimacy infused...with ignorance
Makes four years feel like forty
Believe if ya will...it's all downhill
Willful blindness...evaporates shortly

Delusional...damned and defiled
Where darkness drinks alone
Intelligence whittled to nothing
Mostly just wrinkles and bones

Crooked...career politicians
Corporate money and executive jets
Where incestuous...Capitol cronies...
Only inherit the best

War profiteers...on the ready
To supply all yellow tycoons
Meanwhile the wolves of Wall Street
Are gettin' high...in the champagne rooms

An inauguration of arrogance
Empty suits...and suicide kings
Evil cloaked in patriotism...
Fatted sheep...all ready to scream

WICKED WORDS

As negative emotions
Rip and fray
I choose my words
And fire away
Vulgar...disgusting
Abusive and mean
Neuroscience says
I'm a flawed human being

Stroop Test colors
Defy old taboos
While neural oscillation
Patterns weapons I use
Supernatural swearing
The psychology of words
Where metaphoric mazes
Seem so absurd

Pinker at Harvard
And Bukowski in Women
Describe the graffiti
As they dissect cognition
Where wicked words thunder
Intellectuals cringe
A simpleton...maybe...
I'm still a man among men

KING OF THE IVORIES

Sentenced to three years
In the Missouri State Pen
He was barely five-foot
With sunk...sallow skin

"Assault with intent to rob"
Back in 1923
Sam Hill was the warden...
WOS held the keys

Harry played piano...
In the Missouri Prison Band
He was King of the Ivories
And famous across this land
Nobody played it better...
'Til the Killer came along
Ole Harry was the King...
He smoked it...every song

A five-hundred-watt transmitter
Early in the game
From Canada to Cuba
-n- Great Lakes to the Pontchartrain

"Three O'clock in the Morning"...
To..."Land of My Sunset Dreams"
Harry served eighteen months
Before they set him free

Harry played piano...
In the Missouri Prison Band
He was King of the Ivories
And famous across this land
Nobody played it better...
'Til the Killer came along
Ole Harry was the King...
He smoked it...every song

THIS MOMENT

An elevator repairman
Falls to his death
As a coal miner clings
To life's last breath

A Sherpa surrenders
In the Himalayan cold
While a NASCAR driver's
Heart unfolds

Here in this moment
Ya swear you'll live forever
With no guarantees
Or chance to do things better
There's a single-file line
Stretched across the blue horizon
Here in this moment
We all survive...or die in

Yeah...here in this moment...
We all survive...or die in

A Trooper's vest protects him
From the masked man with a knife
While a nurse saves a baby...
Barely clingin' to life

A lifeguard pulls a surfer
From a rip on Mission Beach
While an airstrike hits its targets
Freein' at least...six Marines

Here in this moment
Ya swear you'll live forever
With no guarantees
Or chance to do things better
There's a single-file line

Stretched across the blue horizon
Here in this moment
We all survive...or die in

Yeah...here in this moment...
We all survive...or die in

HANGIN' CURVEBALL

Karate moves
-n- mosh pit scars
Street cart tacos
And TJ bars

Red Square buzzin'
About A Girl
With bleach blonde hair
-n- Aqua Net curls

His Fender Blues Deluxe
Was stuck on eleven
He wore an Angels' jersey
That said...Blyleven

High speed...lonesome
Like his Stratocaster squall
Never mind Nirvana
Or the hangin' curveball

Yeah...Never mind Nirvana
Or...the hangin' curveball

DETAILS

Don't worry about the details
All "alternative facts" aside
In this land of milk -n- honey
We're a little preoccupied

In the shadows of the gallows
Where the muddy water boils
Don't worry about the details
As we frack more...for our oil

Don't worry about the details
Or earthquakes in Oklahoma
The water in Flint is fine
For lead fueled carcinomas

Addicted to gross distraction
And a marathon of mindless memes
Don't worry about the details
Or how this story ends

No...don't worry about the details
This is how our story ends

DETERIORATE

Cancer cells
-n- guitar swells
Make a man like me...
Uneasy
With my energy gone
It's time to roll on
Thinkin' more...
Since they released me

Eight dollars...in advance
Ten bucks at the door
To watch a man deteriorate
Ya ain't seen me here before

An old Gretsch...is all I've got left
My tone...won't be ignored
So...please watch me deteriorate
Then ya won't see me no more

Yeah...you can watch a man...deteriorate
For ten bucks...at the door

As I sit here wonderin'
Out West it's thunderin'
Ya know...some things never change
This half-assed news
Spells...down home blues
I guess dyin's
Supposed to feel strange

Eight dollars...in advance
Ten bucks at the door
To watch a man deteriorate
Ya ain't seen me here before

An old Gretsch...is all I got left
My tone...won't be ignored

So please watch me deteriorate
Then ya won't see me no more

Yeah...you can watch a man...deteriorate
For ten bucks...at the door

VENTURA

The Dominican Ace
Wore Royal blue
With two-seam speed
Clocked 102
A free agent find
Made power look pretty
He had the meanest leg kick
In Kansas City

Viva Ventura...
Forever fierce and loyal
Painting the outside corner
Powder blue -n- Royal

It's still the early innings...
As your spirit...transcends us all
Oh...Viva Ventura
And the love of a real fastball

Yeah...Viva Ventura
And the love...of a real fastball

A World Series Winner...
Games two and six
He was lean...gasoline
No need for Cueto tricks
Gone at twenty-five...
Ace...now laid to rest
Salvy...Moose and Hos
A Fraternity of Fifteens best

Viva Ventura...
Forever fierce and loyal
Painting the outside corner
Powder blue -n- Royal

It's still the early innings...
As your spirit...transcends us all
Oh...Viva Ventura
And the love of a real fastball

Yeah...Viva Ventura...
And the love...of a real fastball

SWAMP WATER ROSES

Where the Mississippi embayment
Splits North of Crowley's Ridge
There's serious seismic waves
From Cape to New Madrid
You can still hear cannons echo...
Off Chalk Bluff...in early May
Where in...1863
It was Hell...for the Blue -n- the Gray

Swamp Water Roses...
In the early mornin' rain
Hold seeds of soldiers sufferin'...
Their headstones have no names

Old battle songs in the distance
Carry images filled with pain
Yeah...Swamp Water Roses...
In the early mornin' rain

It's...Swamp Water Roses...
And early mornin' rain

In the acidic Southeast soil
Pink blooms can last eight weeks
Fleshy...fertile and fragrant...
As rose hips...sprout new wings
From Crowley's Ridge to Vicksburg
And Natchez to Baton Rouge
Swamp Water Roses...
Are embedded with Delta Blues

Swamp Water Roses...
In the early mornin' rain
Hold seeds of soldiers sufferin'...
Their headstones have no names

Old battle songs in the distance
Carry images filled with pain
Yeah...Swamp Water Roses...
In the early mornin' rain

It's Swamp Water Roses...
And early mornin' rain

WARLORDS OF WASHINGTON

As hungry warmongers
Beat the same old kettle drum
They'll make America slaves...again
While pillagin' the poorest ones...

Buildin' walls on borrowed money
Tradin' souls for foreign oil
It's just another Trumptastrophe
That's already over-boiled

The Warlords of Washington
Are sellin' snake oil by the drum
Convincin' the Christian masses
That we're the chosen ones
How can we trust a Poser...
Who's determined to screw us all
As the Warlords of Washington
Brace for another windfall

Yeah...the Warlords of Washington...
Won't stop...'til they gut us all

Profiteering politicians...
Investment bankers and the privileged few
Don't give a shit...they're all hypocrites...
Ready to turn on me -n- you

Breitbart Nazis...are Kamikazes
Bannon's shenanigans...three doors down
A sadomasochists...strategist
Greasy fingers on a tarnished crown

The Warlords of Washington
Are sellin' snake oil by the drum
Convincin' the Christian masses
That we're the chosen ones
How can we trust a Poser

Determined to screw us all
As the Warlords of Washington
Brace for another windfall

Yeah...The Warlords of Washington
Won't stop...'til they gut us all

WAYLON...WEED & WAFFLES

Waylon sang a Shaver song
Almost as good as Shaver
He made his mark...despite the dark
And his swagger never wavered
There were piles of blow...up his hungry nose
Said he liked the way it smelled
Yeah...Waylon sang a Shaver song
And his records tell the tale

Waylon loved ole Willie
And Willie smoked good weed
Out on tour...there was nothin' cooler
Sold out shows were guaranteed
Every Honky-tonk in Texas
Booked them twelve months in advance
Yeah Waylon loved ole Willie
No matter the circumstance

Waylon loved the Waffle House
And Shooter loved it too
Jessi would go either way
From Lubbock to Kalamazoo
Jessi loved ole Waylon
And he fought like Hell stay
Yeah...Waylon loved good waffles...
Until his dyin' day

Waylon sang a Shaver song
Almost as good as Shaver
He made his mark...despite the dark
And his swagger never wavered
There were piles of blow...up his hungry nose
Said he liked the way it smelled
Yeah...Waylon sang a Shaver song
And his records tell the tale

WETLANDS

They grew up in the South
Northeast of Baton Rouge
Drove a hot rod Chevy Nova
Sixty-Eight...in Fathom blue
Raised on beans -n- bacon
And their Daddy's homemade 'shine
Those boys cheated death...
At least a hundred times

Where the Wetlands meet forever
And time eclipses time
Old gators...lie in wait...
Next to death's trotline

With moonbeams on the water...
Where no one could hear their screams
Down deep in the swamp...Boys...
Just West of New Orleans

Yeah...
Where the Wetlands meet forever...
No one could hear their screams

Rollin' slow...outta Shreveport
South on Forty-Nine
Higher than Uncle Willie
-n- makin' damn good time
Swamp Fox on the radio
Smokin' clove cigarettes
In the heart of Louisiana
Where everything stays wet

Where the Wetlands meet forever
And time eclipses time
Old gators...lie in wait
Next to death's trotline

With moonbeams on the water...
Where no one could hear their screams
Down deep in the swamp...Boys...
Just West of New Orleans

Yeah...
Where the Wetlands meet forever...
No one could hear their screams

PUPPET SHOW

As marionettes of mayhem
Manipulate and maim
Madness is the appointed tool
For minions...so profane
Addicted to constant chaos
Pawns in pinstripe suits
"Alternative facts"...a horse's ass
Determined to kill the truth

Step right up...
To the Puppet Show
Where they'll stop
Hell...no one knows
Pimps...hustlers
Gangsters and thieves
At the Puppet Show
It's cruel deceit

Yeah...this Puppet Show
Is ruled by thieves

Havoc...Hate
And Breitbart spin
Pullin' the strings
On his ignorant friends
Half-assed decisions
Fuel the divide
Like Jim Jones' punch
This is suicide

Step right up...
To the Puppet Show
Where they'll stop
Hell...no one knows
Pimps...Hustlers
Gangsters and thieves

At the Puppet Show
It's cruel deceit

Yeah...this Puppet Show
Is ruled by thieves

GRIZZLY TAINT

Bald eagle perched
In a white pine tree
I'm watchin' him
While he's eyein' me
This Smith 460
Holds five hot rounds
Got my head on a swivel
Just West of Georgetown

In Bear River Valley
Ya better act fast
When a ruthless predator
Is trackin' your ass
Where hollow point power
Either is...or it ain't
Ya don't wanna face
Full of grizzly taint

Yeah...nobody wants
An ole grizzly's taint

Big bull elk
Soakin' up Sun
An ole coyote
Still on the run
Bad boot blisters
Ray-Ban shades
A snort of the Goose
Makes a smooth lemonade

In Bear Creek Valley
Ya better act fast
When a ruthless predator
Is trackin' your ass
Where hollow point power
Either is...or it ain't

Ya don't wanna face
Full of grizzly taint

Yeah...nobody wants
An ole grizzly's taint

RAZOR BURN

As Linda stood in the shower
shaving her long...luscious legs
with a smooth straight razor
in her slathered hand

She was reminded of poor ole Vincent
and how fickle friends can screw you
outside a seedy brothel
just days before Christmas Eve

VISIONS & VINEYARDS

A black crow sits
with knowing eyes
As Visions & Vineyards
smirk at death

Unraveling madness
while tempting more torture
A lying cow
too stoned to care
suffocates the truth

And with straw hat surrendered
he strolls ever-so-slowly
into a bastard's oblivion

SORROW'S TONGUE

As dark voices echo
from Sorrow's Tongue
engulfing unappreciated genius

Artistic Hell-raisers
are often cursed by pretenders
and crudely diagnosed by fools

Yet somehow...they survive

Yes...sorrow speaks
despite the suffering...
in a language only few can comprehend

CYPRESS KNEE

Waving wheat
and a cypress knee

Absinthe breath
with hints of pipe smoke
and inner chaos

Blue paint smudges...
on scuffed Wellington boots

Where mercy died years ago...
and nothingness bleeds forever

GLIMPSE

Two palette knives
on a watchman's chair

Passerine birds
in the absence of light

Impasto-infused suffering
overlooked by the subjectively sane

In the Saint Paul Gardens
slash...142

Where olive trees
wave at death...one more time

And irises...oh the irises
reveal everything...in a fleeting glimpse

ROSE TATTOO

Uncle Mike had a Van Gogh print
on the wall of his detached garage
in Decatur Illinois
He claimed he stole it
from a whorehouse in Mazatlan...
circa 1973

One evenin' after supper...
we got drunk on apricot brandy
and he told me how it all went down

Her name was Alejandra...
she had a skull tattoo on her left ass-cheek
the size of a ripe beefsteak tomato

They screwed twice...
while listenin' to Howlin' Wolf
Truth is...she traded the print to Uncle Mike...
for three Quaaludes and a half spent fifth of red
seven

PALE PINK ROSES

Pale Pink Roses...
Sit silent...in an ancient vase
on a rickety wooden table
Sharing answers to the questions
we're too afraid to ask

Pale Pink Roses...
Reside on the outskirts of Paris
eclipsing raw emotion...
while healing our hurt
between the refractory periods

ORCHARD SHOES

Southern France
in Eighty Eight

A tattered waistcoat
with the third button missing

Exaggerated yellows...
with thousands of black branches

Worn out heels...
on his Orchard Shoes

Rich brown soil...
with traces of oil and turpentine

Thirstier than weathered leather...
splintered impulses raging loudly

Almost ready...for another drink

WORMWOOD ROAD

Staggering slow...
down Wormwood Road
With a loaded revolver
and a ripe...juicy plum

Where dust-devils form
and the realms intersect
You can almost taste the tears...
on the angry faces ya leave behind

LONG SHOT

Pin against primer...
shocking the wheat
A thirty-hour wait
in his thirty-seventh year

If Vincent could've predicted
it would take so goddamned long...
perhaps he might have used congealed blood
to paint his final masterpiece

CHUCK

I can still remember sittin'
on a stack of phone books
in the driver's seat of my Grandma's
'77 Buick LeSabre

Pretendin' it was a sleek
coffee-colored Cadillac
Knowin' in my heart of hearts...
ole Chuck would approve

Fast-forward seventeen years
To the Blue Note in Columbia...
April 17th...1998

Chuck was seventy-one years old...
and didn't appear to
be a day over fourty-five

In a bright blue button down
He was magnificence in action...
Duck walkin' and shit talkin'
just like I'd always imagined

It was the first and only time
I saw him perform live...
and I should have my ass
kicked sideways for that

I guess I must have wanted
to freeze-frame time

Because that night
in Columbia Missouri
The King of Rock N' Roll
took us all to school

SMOKE

Eatin' my smoke
From a bright colored packet
Fannin' these flames
In my corduroy jacket

Whiskey stopped workin'
And the pills are no use
I'll cleanse all my sins
When I remember the truth

Sensible solutions
For everyday pain
Eatin' my smoke
While fannin' the flames

Hallucinogenic Half-life
Mail-order magic
I'll share the address
If ya think you can hack it

SUZY

Suzy has a stack
of dusty chapbooks
sittin' on a turquoise TV tray...
next to the tattered tan recliner
in her livin' room

She used to relish reviewin'
every single release
Now Suzy just sits...
starin' into the sensational abyss

Wonderin' why words are wicked...
and the water she's been walkin' on
suddenly feels so warm

CINDY

I met her in
the men's room
at Sandstone
on August 4th, 1999

She was pissin'
in the sink
while shoutin' out the
words to..."You Got Lucky"

Cindy had dirty
dishwater hair
and the longest...tannest
legs I'd ever seen

The brand of beautiful
that induces seizures
in slackers like me

I knew Cindy was
way outta my league
but that night
I was just stoned enough
to step up to the plate

About that time
Campbell hit a greasy lick...

and I went down Swingin'

BRENDA

Brenda drove
a Viagra-blue
Olds Cutlass Supreme
that she inherited
from her Grandma

It had a ding in the
driver's side door
and the headliner was
comin' unraveled at the seam

We'd go parkin'
on Ole Number Eight sometimes
and have to wait twenty minutes
for the windows
to defog

Brenda had mad skills
the kind of talent
folks pay big money to see
on the silver screen

We lost touch after High School...

Last I heard...
She's somewhere on the Left Coast
married to a guy...half my age...
worth just shy of twenty million

SHERRI'S S-10 CHEVY

Scott sweet talked Sherri
out of her S-10 Chevy...
shortly after the LA Riots
in 1992

We left San Diego
searchin' for somethin'
that I'm still not sure
we ever found

I'll never forget
the smell of the smolderin' city
And the stunned looks
on faces we saw...
Standin' along the streets
in Compton and Watts

We were just two crazy ass
white dudes...
in Sherri's slick
S-10 Chevy

I remember askin' Scott
to speed up or slow down
at least ten separate times

Knowin' in the heartbeat of
that moment...
We'd never be the same

SNAPPY'S

She stuck her tongue
down my throat
at Snappy's Tavern
during finals' week
in 1997

It was the first semester
of Nursing School...
so Anatomy & Physiology
were certainly our
highest priorities

She had beautiful brown eyes
and a deep...dark tan
that reminded me of a
summer fling with Sara
in San Diego...
just six years before

Most days after class
we'd slip out to Crowder Lake
in my '88 Fleetwood
so we could study
in private

She sure had me hooked
for a few fun filled months
until I met her Husband
one Sunday at Snappy's...
and never spoke to her again

DEBBIE

Debbie drove
a black-panel van
that her Dad had picked
up at an auction
in Alma

She said it was
previously owned
by the local funeral home
and only used
for out-of-state runs
when their hearse was
tied up

I always wondered
if Debbie could hear
unsettled spirits laughin'
when she'd take
her dealer parkin'
down by the river

Debbie ran faster than most....
so I can only imagine
the stories she'd tell today
if she hadn't taken that hot dose
in the summer of '98

BONEYARD BREAKFAST

Black currant blood
from a hand-painted flask

Razorback chops
on old cast iron

Ditch water coffee...
and gooseberry jam

Just another
Boneyard Breakfast...

For the haunted hungry
in hell's kitchen

BEGGARS' BRANDY

Sippin' Applejack Brandy
on Blackhorse Row
There's no tiles left
in the boneyard

I sit in silence
too scared to surface
Certain that they're still searchin'...
In fear they'll finally find me

So with a belly full
of beggars' brandy...
I'll smoke my last pack
of Djarum Blacks

And await
the executioner

TRIPPIN'

He said—
In order to use your head
ya gotta escape your mind

So I smoked...
shot and snorted
almost everything
over the past decade

He said—
Buy the ticket
and take the ride...
Trippin' might work wonders

So I sacrificed...
suffered and sold my soul
so many times...
This scarred shell is all that's left

Almost empty
and too tired for sleep
I can still hear his voice echo
when the moon is full

He says—
Stay the course Kid
This journey...
while temporary
is truly tremendous

Especially...when you're trippin'

TURQUOISE CHOKER

The night she first spoke to me
I was slow sippin' single malt
at Two Fools Tavern
in Albuquerque

She wore a sultry
yellow sundress
and silver -n- turquoise choker

There were hints of
sandalwood and sadness
as I traced her soft supple skin
with a smooth...steady hand

We made our way
to my silver Seville
just in time
to see the sun comin' up

It was early that Sunday mornin'
when she smiled at me and said...

This silver -n- turquoise choker
belonged to my Sister Sara
in San Diego

She wanted me to tell ya...
She thinks you've suffered enough

BAG-BRIDE

I met Ashley
on December 8th, 1991
She was standin' outside
the Greyhound Station
in Milwaukee

Saint Paul Avenue
was seriously snow-packed
and the reported wind-chill
was at minus eleven

Ashley was shiverin'
like a Shar Pei shittin' peach seeds
so I offered her my pea coat
which she graciously accepted
without hesitation

As she slowly puffed
another Parliament
I asked her why
Wisconsin in the wintertime

Ashley said she'd been
a Bag-Bride...back in Boston
and that her pimp
would never dream
of lookin' for her
on Lake Michigan

When my Checker cab
finally arrived...
I handed her my card
and said keep the coat

It's gonna get a lot colder
when winter sets in

137

CABRINI-GREEN

We took a Checker Cab
to the North side of Chicago
on September 14th, 1991

Conway was convinced
it would be cool
to slow troll through
Cabrini-Green

As we exited the cab
on West Division Street
every hair on the back of my neck
stood at attention

We were walkin' and talkin'
for less than a block
when a blue -n- white police cruiser
pulled up and motioned us over

Their passenger-side window
was barely cracked...
as the officer ridin' shotgun said
"Get in the back...NOW"

Cabrini-Green was known
for two things in the early '90's....
Murder and Misery

We saw gang signs...graffiti
and sweet smoke rollin'
from screen-less windows
where hungry tenants
were barbecuin' in their bathtubs

When Chicago's Finest
dropped us off at Navy Pier
we caught the next Checker
and never considered cruisin'
Cabrini-Green again

PHOENIX

The night we got pulled over
in Phoenix
we were trollin' for fresh talent
on Van Buren Street

Earlier that afternoon
Perkins had boosted a rented Lincoln
from the dipshit valet...
at Royal Palms

So after we'd spent some serious coin
at the Candy Store
we decided to see what
the rest of the city had to offer at 3AM

Our first stop was the Circle K
where Perkins liberated four tallboys...
A fistful of Slim Jims
and two King Size Snickers

He moonwalked down every aisle
while I flirted with the tweaker chick...
chompin' her Blue Blowout Bubblicious
behind bulletproof glass

Ten minutes later...
a Phoenix Police cruiser
lit our Lincoln up like
a fireworks finale on the Fourth of July

They had us sprawled out
on the warm city sidewalk
until we got our story straight

as the sun was comin' up
just before their shift change

In that one magnificent moment
on August 17th, 1996
We were the luckiest motherfuckers
to ever arrive at the Royal Palms
with a full police escort

BURNAM ROAD

A little white house
with detached garage

The smell of
chocolate chip cookies
mixed with Jiffy Pop

Dr. Pepper fizz dancin'
from a Hong Kong Phooey cup

Watchin' Star Trek reruns
with Uncle Mike

Fawn and Brindle
Boxer puppies

Aunt Mary's long black hair
filled with stardust
and hints of coconut shampoo

A Lone Ranger sleepin' bag
sprawled out across
their avocado green
shag carpet

I'm forty-four years old now....
and still drive by
the little white house
on Burnam Road

Wishin' I were six again...

Hopin' these memories
will refuse to fade
for at least another forty years

RATTLESNAKE BONES

Coyote tracks
in the creek bank mud

A bellyful of
Old Overholt

Down to my
last few doses

Still searchin' for salvation
in the Triplett Timber

Where sun-bleached
rattlesnake bones

And petrified
morel mushrooms

Know more about sufferin'
than they'll ever tell me

ROOSTER

Our cocky-ass rooster
and crazy black cat
would chase each other
for hours on end

The ole rooster
sized up his opponent
long before Carlos The Cat
ever caught on

It was usually
a magnificent match
until one fateful Sunday
in late February

When Roberto...
The Rooster
ended up
on our rotisserie

And Carlos licked his chops
waitin' on rooster remains...
in warm milk gravy

FRIENDLY SKIES

Fly the friendly skies
they say...
What's the worst
thing that could happen

Rug burn...
A fractured femur...
Crushed clavicle
Or an old school pistol whippin'

Think I'll start savin' now
for a first class upgrade....

Hell...
I might even take
five free Kung Fu lessons
at Lee's Chinese Martial Arts

They say San Francisco
is beautiful this time of year...

But I'm nowhere near ready
for a title fight...
on the red-eye flight

When some skeleton crew
wants to bump me...
so they can deadhead
out to Denver

JEFF

The night we
crushed the guardrail
in Jeff's '88 Iroc-Z
we'd been drinkin'
at a Tiki Bar
on Del Mar Beach
all afternoon

When the first State Trooper
arrived on the scene
he claimed Jeff's speedometer
froze on impact at 102

I'll never forget the smell
of purple racin' fuel
on sunbaked concrete
or the taste of
bourbon-infused blood
tricklin' down the back of my throat

I still consider myself
somewhat lucky...
since I walked away

Jeff was much less fortunate...
He hasn't been able
to feel his legs
since April 12th, 1992

CHARLIE

A big bowl
of Bruce Banner
from a hand-blown bong

Prince servin' pineapple pancakes
with purified purple drink...
filtered fresh...from Lake Minnetonka

Micki sinkin' free throws
from fifteen feet
while the rest of the Revolution
rinse and repeat

You can sleep deep now
Charlie Murphy...

Ole Dave's back at the wheel

TIN SHED

There were
baseball-sized dents
on the North side
of Grandpa's tin shed

Our field was surrounded
by two separate fencerows
and thirty acres of soybeans
that measured 215 feet
to dead center

We played weekly
during warm weather months
Typically losin' at least
three baseballs a game...
to tall fescue
along the perimeter

It's been more than thirty years
since we last graced
our makeshift
field of dreams

Grandpa's been gone fifteen...

Yet almost every Sunday
I wake up with
the same excited feelin'

Wishin' it was still '77...
and I could swing
that sweet
Louisville Slugger again

SHAWN

The night they shot Shawn
in the stomach
outside Wicked Ways
tattoo shop
in San Antonio

I was shootin' eight ball
at Slick Willie's
Wonderin' why
it was takin' him so long
to come pick me up

Witnesses said...
Shawn screamed for help
just seconds before
they shot him the second time
with a sawed-off twelve

I'll never forget
the poem Ginger read
at his closed casket
as we all grieved for Shawn
in our own ways

I struggled to make sense of it
for sixteen solitary years
carryin' an indescribable
pressure in my chest

They finally executed
the bastards
who slaughtered Shawn...

And despite what scripture says...
I was ready to see them go

MEDIOCRE MASS

Easter Mass
was mediocre this year
At the Holy Name of Jesus
Catholic Church and bingo hall

From genuflection
to resurrection
Father Michael seemed
somewhat melancholy

His half-hearted homily
held our attention
for approximately
five minutes

Sister Rose shook her head
from side to side
as the smoldering incense
reminded her of a Steppenwolf
concert in Saskatchewan
circa 1968

The silver lining
as far as I'm concerned
was when I skimmed some
Holy Water...from the fancy font
in back

Most Easter mornings
I wake up parched
and while the whiskey
is wearing off...
holy hydration
can taste almost heavenly

K.W.Peery

ABOUT THE ILLUSTRATOR

Bruce McClain is a political cartoonist, illustrator, animation design artist, poet, and veteran Marine. He's spent time in his career both in New York and California, and is now living in the Midwest. He studied at the Phoenix School of Design before receiving an offer to join the animation team for the feature animated film, The War Wizards, a Ralph Bakshi production in California. During this time, McClain interned with the American animation studio, Hanna Barbera.

While in Los Angeles, Mr. McClain studied under the tutelage of the animation genius, Johnny Vita who was a pioneer in the form. Bruce also attended night classes at UCLA cartooning under Matt Wurker, a political cartoonist for major newspapers. Around this time, Bruce packaged his own animated concept into a Made-For-Television project, Valley of the Mushroom Patch, presented at the Preview House in Los Angeles.

Bruce McClain resides in Blue Springs, MO and is busy creating art and honing a new love for poetry.

Made in the USA
San Bernardino, CA
12 August 2017